Chairlift Philosopher

Chairlift Philosopher
Ski Trip

DUNCAN CULLMAN

LitPrime Solutions
21250 Hawthorne Blvd
Suite 500, Torrance, CA 90503
www.litprime.com
Phone: 1 (209) 788-3500

© 2021 Chairlift Philosopher. All rights reserved.

No part of this book may be reproduced, stored in a retrieval system, or transmitted by any means without the written permission of the author.

Published by LitPrime Solutions   05/05/2021

ISBN: 978-1-954886-14-8(sc)
ISBN: 978-1-954886-15-5(e)

Library of Congress Control Number: 2021902979

Any people depicted in stock imagery provided by iStock are models, and such images are being used for illustrative purposes only.

Certain stock imagery © iStock.

Because of the dynamic nature of the Internet, any web addresses or links contained in this book may have changed since publication and may no longer be valid. The views expressed in this work are solely those of the author and do not necessarily reflect the views of the publisher, and the publisher hereby disclaims any responsibility for them.

Composed on St Rosa de Lima Day
while in La Punta Callao, PE

Table of Contents

- From Orphan In A Basket To Child In His Garden 1
- Eight Years Old And The Ark 4
- Visions Of The Green Prince (OF Lund) On Midsummer Night: Green Leaves Blooming 6
- Umbilical Cord 10
- Roadmap Of Male And Female And The Source 12
- Dear God, ... 14
- Dear God Two 17
- Peace In The Streets 19
- A Timeless Jew And The Traffic Cop, The Kingdom Of Heaven Is Like… 22
- Our Love 25
- Your New Commandment Makes Many, At Least In All: The New Earth 27
- Chairlift Philosopher 29
- St. Littletown 31
- Stowe 33
- The Great Man Is Here Again 35
- Daddy's Gone Away 38
- Our Time Will Come Again 42
- While There Is Still Time 43
- Last Summer Read All About It, Extra Extra 46
- Surprise 48
- Martyrs For A Green Planet 49

- ❖ Sainthood 51
- ❖ Booby Trap Nation 53
- ❖ Israel 56
- ❖ Wide Is The Abyss 58
- ❖ Marta's House 60
- ❖ Epidemic 62
- ❖ Marielle 64
- ❖ Ski Racer 69
- ❖ Abandoned 70
- ❖ Arlene 75
- ❖ Your Blanket 77
- ❖ The Garden 79
- ❖ Kingdom 82
- ❖ Boy From Ipanema 84
- ❖ Dorothy And Louis In Portillo 86
- ❖ Chanukah Poem 89
- ❖ Slow Freddy 91
- ❖ We Follow Jesus In Our Procession 93
- ❖ Study The Book Of Life Like A Hebrew Even If You Are Not One, Just Imagine You Could Be 96
- ❖ Othmar 98
- ❖ The Duke 101
- ❖ Listen To The Word Of God That He Is Good 104
- ❖ Slalom Hill Portillo Was North Facing (Pomalift Hill) 107
- ❖ St. Ullrich 109
- ❖ Dear God Three 112
- ❖ Now That God Is Dead 114
- ❖ Judgement Day, Elohim 120

From Orphan In A Basket To Child In His Garden

God has recalled His very dearest son

Who was sacrificed to become His Lamb

One who has died for all our sins

In order that we might be redeemed and forgiven

We are homeless, we are orphans

We were chosen by no one, we were abandoned

Left in the desolation to wander

Left among the nations destined for destruction

We were in a sheep herd led by black sheep, like the Bedouin

Even so, God offers us redemption and forgiveness

Our One God invites us to come home

We need no longer wander like lost children

We may be adopted into the royal family of God

Whose special beloved son was Jesus the messiah crucified

Abandoned by his nation and disciples to die
alone upon the cross on Golgotha Hill

That all the orphans (huerfanos) and homeless, even traitors

Be brought back into the circle of love and forgiven if they ask

You who are homeless and afraid

Wander no longer with the Jackals in desolate places

For our Redeemer is here now, come and join the wedding banquet

Sup with the Lamb in heaven, dine with the Royal Family of God

Find your refuge in Christ who is risen for your sake

That where he has gone to prepare a room for you

Rise up with your newfound wings to be angels on high

Sing hallelujah and praise

For God is omnipotent and forgets not the orphans and widows

Those whose hearts cry out for mercy unto our Lord

Will find shelter from the storm, He will
wrap us in a warm blanket of love

He will bring us home to salvation

Though we suffer when we forget Him

CHAIRLIFT PHILOSOPHER

He has remembered us and embraces our return through prayer

Our Father Who is in heaven as well as on Earth

Thy kingdom come Thy will be done

Hallowed be Thy name

We who are all prodigal sons and daughters daily

"You are all My children"

"Swing on your swing sets swing high up into
the Apple Tree to Me your God"

"I will catch you (My Son) like your mother like your father"

"I will catch you and not let you fall, have faith in Me"

Thus says the Father of fathers, a Judge (for the Mother
of mothers, the Holy Spirit and Physician)

Saint Rose of Lima has revealed this to me
from a cloud so I wrote this for you

From the Garden of the New Jerusalem

Eight Years Old
And The Ark

I was still a child and eight years old when my father and I were invited by my uncles and cousins to go to a Hebrew Synagogue on the upper west side of New York not to far north of Central Park but northerly enough to be influenced by Haarlem which had become an African-American neighborhood. We took a taxi there. I remember it as being early autumn.

I considered myself a baseball player at the time with a bright future in Little League. We had great coaches with moral values. I played for the catholic team the Knights of Columbus but in a few years I would change to the Kiwanis team sponsored by the Masons, I cannot remember exactly as I was more interested in the game of baseball, Mickey Mantle, Yogi Berra and Roger Maris of the New York Yankees.

So we all crowded into this apartment and over by the piano, well it looked like a piano but it was golden, a big mysterious looking thing. I have never seen anything like that ever since or before.

Don t look at it my father warned me

So we went to our seats and someone turned out the lights. And my cousins who were devoted Hebrews warned me not to open my eyes because God was going to come out of that contraption and would kill us if we dared to open our eyes.

And someone said that maybe it wasn't working at all.

And someone else said to be quiet God was just not yet sure about us that we had to be more sincere

We waited. If God was coming out of that box there was no way I was going to miss the show and suddenly as I opened my eyes a light came crawling out of the box and saw my open eyes uh-oh.

I passed out cold.

There were creatures of all shapes and sizes of all creations in all planets all seraphim and I was totally afraid like never in my entire life and then came some cherubim and perhaps some angels.

I lay on the floor when the lights came back on in the room but I was still unconscious there surrounded by my unbelieving cousins including Susan who said something to the effect that I must have opened my eyes and was indeed dead

Suddenly I woke up from my spell and I had not seen God but had seen too much and had been terribly afraid but now I was overjoyed to see my cousins laughing at me.

Visions Of The Green Prince (OF Lund) On Midsummer Night: Green Leaves Blooming

Visions of the Green Prince who sees green leaves blooming

The long night of human madness

Must end or man will perish

So now must come the dawn of human awakening

The system of greed and pollution must be compromised

Or the planet will become something we no longer recognize as our own

Since we will not even exist.

While traveling abroad I have been reborn in spirit

At the prospect of world green revolution

Because corporate greed

Is destroying our way of a healthy lifestyle.

CHAIRLIFT PHILOSOPHER

The USA has become the sickest dog

In the pack of hounds running wildly

People are encouraged there

Not to walk or bicycle but to drive fast luxury cars

To Walmart where they park in Handicap Parking and

Ride electric wheelchairs through the endless aisles

Because they have lost the use of their feet.

This lifestyle of heart attack stroke and cancer

Must be averted by the followers and proponents of the Green Revolution

And this mindless architecture of misadventure needs be taken back to the drawing board and recreated by

Proponents of Life not Death!

So what needs to be done is for the people to seize their governments

Take control of their governments

Be responsible for themselves

This will not be an easy task.

Individually we cannot accomplish much politically.

We will need to create a worldwide party in this endeavor.

Each of us was once lost in the darkness of material consumption

From this we fell ill

Became depressed and burdened

By anxiety.

But now we see the light

It is bright and shining

Like the Sun.

We will raise high our Green Standards (Banners)

This world is not just for corporate CEOs

It is our world too,

We must take it back!

There is a green Prince or Princess in each and every one of us

We must look inside ourselves

To find the strength to rid ourselves and the planet

Of this corporate plague.

We must have government of the people

For the people.

So help us God that we as a Green Nation of the living

Do not perish in a perishing world,

Because Life is essential to us,

Therefore raise high your Green Banner of Truth and the Way.

CHAIRLIFT PHILOSOPHER

Be of clean conscience and be cleansed

There are people like Bernie Sanders whom we endorse,

He is a prophet

Before his time,

So are We.

The proponents of Big Business do not like to hear

What we have to say

Because the Gargantuan Hospitals

Will go broke without patients.

Here at the Lund Train station

There are three thousand bicycles

So this might be considered

The capitol of something very good brewing

The Wind is shifting in Our Direction

And like brave Vikings

We shall all raise Our green Mast and Sail.

God be with Us and against those who destroy the Planet!

After All Our Health is more important than wealth

Umbilical Cord

That man cannot comprehend God and no woman needs to be afraid

Therefore we have Jesus Christ as God's chosen representative (and the Virgin Mother Mary)

A man attached by an unseen umbilical cord to God, his Father

If we so believe in Him we shall not perish but have everlasting life

Whereby we shall also have unseen umbilical cords to God, our true Father of all our fathers

Whereby God who has both mercy and love for us shall forgive us our sins

We have sinned and broken laws given to us for our protection

We were speeding on the highway to our lust thinking we would not be caught

However God knows everything and what is in our hearts and minds

Please restore my parental umbilical cord in some unseen fashion Lord

That I may continue to be obedient to all my fathers and mothers back to Adam, Eve and You

Because I know You are the Power in my life if I shall be allowed to live one more day

In order to sing psalms of salvation by You alone no other, Selah

Roadmap Of Male And Female And The Source

How important it is to pray

And for those who may have speech impediments let them write to our One God

O please dear God give us a road map

Let us imagine that you convert bad energy into good when it passes through You

Hate and destruction are consumed in Your Holy Fire and converted

Into a Holy Ghost of pure love be it female perhaps at 12 o'clock it descends into the universes

By six o'clock it is corrupted somewhat and becomes male energy, it becomes like human ego

Here we find George Washington and Moses in charge of empire

Due to temptation this egoistical adventure becomes misadventure

By nine o'clock we have corporate greed, at ten o'clock fatchism and communism

By eleven o'clock we have world war and total destruction, by 11:59 we have Armageddon

Because the pure love of God is mistaken for weakness and mismanaged

Humans are each both male and female except in the case of Hitler who decided against his mother and grandmother, and against love itself (God also)

Jesus came to us from one o'clock, maybe in the afternoon, the right hand of our very God midnight

If in fact midnight to noon is the Id itself and unconscious

Then so

Kindergarten and sleep are at three o'clock but nightmares are the eleven o'clock news?

So charity is at four o'clock and philanthropists are at five thirty

So how am I, personally, to avoid this very trap of egoism so prevalent in this world?

How shall I be reborn and innocent of all this corruption and hatred in this extreme planet of lies?

How will I accept only the Truth and not be fooled? I must be vigilant and watchful. I must Trust that my God shall lead me into his greener pastures.

For I was like a lost sheep but the Good Shepherd came to look for me! Hallelujah Amen

Dear God,

Dear God, Robert says it's too late for us to be saved as we ignored the Messiah and the King, and especially Your commandments and laws, RSVSVP.

Dear Descendants of Abraham,

Why don't you learn like Abraham did?

Learn to follow your inner voice, learn to walk in the path of righteousness

Trust in Me your one God, I will lead you to the heavenly stream

Into the Garden of righteousness that you might know the Truth

That I am Who I am, that I am your God, so walk with Me

For I will lead you correctly in the way and the truth, there is no other

So respond to those who call you, I have sent them

To be your friends that you may confess to them that I have sent you forth

To proclaim liberty to the captives, to feed the hungry and house orphans

To hold up a lantern in the darkness for the lost, let My white light shine forth

Though it may blind those who are drunk, others will see

See that your God is the only way and bow down in service to Me

It is not about us, it is about Me, I am that I am, it is not for you to know

The mind of your God is too magnificent for you to even imagine

My thoughts are far more numerous than even all the atoms in your material universe

You cannot comprehend me, but marvel at my power, that I have created you

From dust and star dust, so trust in Me, that I alone am the Good

What is in your world is both good and bad, it is in the mind of the beholder

What he or she shall see is a reflection of one's own faith

If there is no purpose to your life then you shall lose it, for I am the grand plan

Come to Me and live, for I am life itself and the life everlasting

If you will just abide in Me then I will so abide in you

Therefore you will walk in clarity and clairvoyance into Truth where I am

You shall be also for I have spoken it through the ages, My every Word

Is My promise to you who believe in me lest you disbelieve

Then darkness shall cover you like the waves of the sea you shall be engulfed in ruin

You need not despair for I am here if you shall ask for Me say

My very dearest of all, God in heaven and on earth

Please enter the temple of my body to fill me with your Holy Spirit of Love

That I may see the Truth and confess that You are my only God

There is no other, i let everything go in order to come to You

For You alone shall restore to me all I need daily and every minute of my life, every second

Now I belong to You alone and so You shall abide in me, thus I shall live in You and You in me

Therefore you shall be My sons and daughters, all sisters and brothers in Me, your heavenly Father and Mother too for I am Everything do pray

Dear God Two

Dear God too let me confess your holy name to Robert in Argentina

He suffers so for Your sake and to glorify You

Dearest my one and only God, let me worship no other without penalty

But I want to walk in righteousness so raise me up from my couch

To encounter You to meet You on Your highway

Our relationship together, you and I could be in no other fashion because God controls our destiny

It has all been planned in advance to turn out this way

Because our loving One and Only has decreed and ordained EVERYTHING

I did not create myself and neither did you, for God has created us from stardust

Dear Robert, I have pleaded with our One and Only Dearest and His Her Its response

Without our pain and suffering we may not enter Your Grace and Humility

They cast lots for Your clothing, they mixed wine with Your water

They humiliated our One and Only so we might also to enter Your Covenant

Your Law is for our protection and safety, You clothe us in righteousness

We walk only because of You and find our only rest in You

May Robert walk Your walk and may Robert sleep and rest in You

Bring the blanket of Your Covenant to warm him in winter and a shade tree to cool him in summer

We need to take smaller bites of our food because You are our nourishment

You have brought us into this our undeniable destiny to glorify You Alone

Senior Soledad, Mt Lonely on Your Tree of righteousness

There was no other way to bring you and me to Grace but by this our present paths

Understandably we suffer for the cause of Your Glory to be seen within us

We forgive You, Lord God Who forgives us our trespasses with undying love

It is Your Holy Spirit which invades us joyfully we sing in praise and exaltation

We lift our voices and our hearts to You our One and Only Dearest the Source of all creation

Prayer for Robert and Myriam

Peace In The Streets

The Day of Peace

On that Day of Peace

When cars are banned

From ten till four

The people will awaken

By using their feet

They shall rediscover one another

Fresh new faces

On horses, bicycles, skates and skis

It will be a whole New World.

Ambulances school buses fire and police cars

Will be used with limitations

But there will be for the most part

Peace on the Earth

From ten till four

Both Night and Day

Because our Earth and We

Need a break from this madness

I was a very young boy

In a hurricane 1953

We lost electricity and cooked in our fireplace

Yet it was the closest my family ever became

Perhaps there shall be

Huge parking garages

Near Interstate exits

And interstate highway travel

Will be allowed more travel hours

Two till twelve?

But overall

This current madness will cease

CHAIRLIFT PHILOSOPHER

I will see you smile

And shake your hand

I could never do that

Through a windshield

A Timeless Jew And The Traffic Cop, The Kingdom Of Heaven Is Like...

Our God on his throne in heaven

The timeless original Jew his mind unlike our own he knows everything everywhere

We just imagine we know everything and we fake it then doubt ourselves

Why do we doubt ourselves? There is no good reason to doubt that God exists

There are bosses everywhere and captains of each ship so follow the rules

Where do these rules of law spring from to preserve and protect us?

Someone must love us like our mother and father when we were born!

The timeless Jew on His Throne beyond the clouds and lightning

He is directing all the traffic like a street cop at the intersection of highways

There are some impatient frustrated road rage drivers who shouldn't be armed and dangerous

The IRA and second amendment guarantees their rebellion

They brandish their pistols at other drivers to try and get through to nowhere fast

Imagining that there is no God at all just a cheese soufflé at a Christmas Party

The traffic cop has always arrived at these times of congestion when the light fails

Why don't you see the light? It is red, yellow and green? There is the big white light too!

There is a hole in the sky and here comes a thunderbolt in the massive downpour!

Now the windshield wipers are of no use at all, there is a cloudburst of righteousness

You have woken up finally so unload your gun the cop is here to protect you with the law

Your taxes are at work, that's why you pay them, for protection against your passion

Because you were carried away in your hatred of that timeless Jew at the synagogue

He is hidden from you since you are an unbeliever you cry out,

"I hate those bastards!" Yes you hate God also and so you have cursed yourself as well

Your whole day is ruined by this cop at the intersection who has come to save you from a terrific accident

Why is it you are so accident prone and self-destructive? You hate this and you hate that!

You hate the traffic cop and the red light as well, and your coffee needs cream and sugar

You hate the rising gas prices and the inflation at the supermarket

You hate what's on television and you hate the news and you even hate your own life, don't you?

You are sick of this and that and now you have fallen ill and gone to the Hospital...

When will you learn? You hated school and dropped out of that too to get a better job with more stress in awful working conditions

After a long life you lost your good looks but now at least you are the big boss

You must have done something right somewhere to earn this greater responsibility?

The traffic cop is still out there on the highway, there's been a terrible accident, and it's someone you know as you drive by them tell you the news...

Hate no more because hatred kills, and speed no more because speed kills...

There are laws and there will be justice, whoever caused this accident will be sent to prison for drunk driving and homicide

The traffic cop knows you and knows where you must be going

Trust Him, Trust in Him who is sent to deliver you, we trust in God the Almighty because He is our Savior, Amen

Our Love

In this morbid world there is disease, pestilence and plague

But under the canopy of your love

I am now among the anointed

As though my covenant with you

Is given by God and is a covenant with the Lord most high.

Many waves pound upon our shore,

There are those who do not believe God is good,

And do not receive love just hate instead

They are bitter toward us and jealous

Because we are a mighty Citadel,

A mountaintop castle among the clouds

Majestic and high with waterfalls

That fall from Zion. Our love

DUNCAN CULLMAN

Is like a limitless fountain

It gushes forth abundantly from hidden springs

To bring us joy this Holiday season

And shine like a beacon of hope, a lighthouse

For many still lost upon the sea of despair

Your New Commandment Makes Many, At Least In All: The New Earth

Your new commandment is to love not hate your adversary. Yes to love your enemy

So call him or her Saint Adversary because if you shall hate him you will fear him also and lose the fight

He or she is given to you by God that you may have courage else wise you might become a spineless wimp

So say St Adversary, I am thankful to you (Osama Bin Laden, Hitler, Stalin, Khmer Rouge, Trump) it will not profit you to hate and fear, so love instead!

Now go to your friends who are also greater Saints and think of them as such as they were sent by God to you also. St. Comrades.

Therefore call the place you live in Heaven because your town is now St. Town and your homeland is St. Country and St. Nation

St. United Nations we will be under St. Justice because you love now therefore you will be free

Free from fear and free from hate and free from bondage in the New Promised St. Land where even you will become a Saint, St. You and St. Me in Heaven on St. Our Planet

Chairlift Philosopher

The kingdom of heaven is like a chairlift philosopher: he rides the chairlift into the sky.

He hopes God is there above him in the clouds above to protect him from avalanches, falling rocks, wolves, bears and gravity.

He thinks that perhaps he is living too selfish a life as a freestyle competitor; that he should go back to school and study to become a teacher. He studies the landscape, the blue white moon of high altitude, visible in the daytime.

His life on the summit is lonely, the other competitors don't befriend him much. He is no more selfish than any other man because all are. He only needs to confide in God to have a friend, the God of his father's and grandfather's. There is only one God.

He remembers walking in New York City. A man in a white robe was there, a Mohammed in, a Muslim. So he asked the man,

"What must I do to follow your one God, Allah?"

The man replied,

"You must give up everything to follow Allah!"

"Even my skis? I am a skier?" This perplexed him.

"Even your skis, everything! "Replied the man with authority.

The skis are on my feet; must I give up even my feet as well he wondered still while overlooking distant peaks and busy valleys.

"I am like a condor!" thought the chairlift philosopher who decided not to give up his wings. So he continued to soar among the high snow-capped peaks.

Continue to be whatever you are for God has given you all this talent for your own niche in survival. It is your purpose under heaven to be helpful to the world's economy. Try to be helpful. If you are a general then lead your army. God in heaven will rectify everything. He will smash into pieces the wicked. If you obey His commandments you might hopefully be spared. Yet He cannot spare you from death in this lowly existence in this material world. Everything that lives here must die. She will wrap Her great wings around you and lift you up into Her bosom which is heaven.

She is like your mother, a loving God and like your father forgiving though sterner.

Worship no other

St. Littletown

It's more imperative that we focus on and appreciate what we have

What God has ordained for us here and now

Rather than upon what we don't have though we might want more (covet)

For the kingdom of heaven is like an unhappy man living in a small town

He looks around him and criticize everyone and everything he sees,

So he exclaims,

"What a wretched little town this is, so very small, and everyone here is a loser!"

It is his own shortsightedness for belittling his tiny town.

It would be better for him to rename his tiny town "St. Littleton"

Because every street corner is full of potential Saints.

Such a rotten world we live in if we think it so

Yet in the eyes of God it is His Perfection and His Plan

That we rise up and overcome to be the heroes He wants us to be.

We are all potentially His Saints in the making through His Grace

We are reformed only by trial and tribulation.

Thus we each fight a personal Armageddon daily!

My brother and sister Saints now I behold your struggles,

If I were only better able to discern and see your Saintliness in the making

Then I might become a happier man and be more gleeful and Saintly.

"Oh, my dear Saintly brothers and sisters, how I empathize with your mundane daily struggles,

In the final Day we shall all be brothers and rise together to meet God our wonderful Creator

Such great joy will this be and I am now confident in everyone I meet that he or she is sent by you, God, to help me fulfill my role in Your Grand Plan

Stowe

For me when I was young Stowe was some mysterious foreign place where white rich people wore mink coats and arrived in limousines. I went there to ski one weekend when my father was too busy in New York so he sent me with Milton Hewitt, a really tough New Yorker kind of a guy. He looked like he could have been an FBI agent and probably was but his daughter was Millie, a nice gullible girl a few years my senior. Maybe she was fifteen and she had a crush on Marvin Moriarity, the son of the local hat maker, he was an aspiring downhill ski racer about to make the Olympic team. She looked for his ski tracks in the snow.

"Marven has been here", said Millie

"See those straight ski tracks like figure elevens, he schusses everything!"

So we skied very fast trying to catch up with Marvin but he was much too fast and Millie eventually married someone else from Stowe but not Marvin who moved to Florida later in life with some hot rich blonde tennis star. They still play tennis there and in Stowe in summertime.

I was in tears after being chewed out by Millie's father because I was cold having not brought enough warm clothing. He realized the mistake and comforted me that I was not that bad a kid after all, but he was lying so that I would stop crying on the seven hour car ride back to Connecticut

I slept solidly as the car heater felt like the second coming of our Lord and savior.

So I never went back to Stowe after that until age eighteen with Connie Hendricks in her Volkswagen bug. She was such a sweet blond young lady from Oberlin College in Ohio and her father was an associate of my grandfather MacBride somehow who lived in a house in the middle of the road Hudson, New Hampshire. Eventually the state straightened that main highway and the house was gone so was her father too. But Connie brought me to Stowe so we could race in the very prestigious Stowe Cup won by Billy Kidd and Marvin Moriarity etc.

Connie announced to me that she would be staying with her boyfriend maybe Eric Reid, a Dartmouth ski racer, so could she drop me off at some motel? I confessed I had only one dollar and she said I could stay with the Catholic lady in her burlap bunk room at her house which featured no sheets on the beds and mostly late night drunks and bums with the influenza. I relented and let her have her way as she picked me up seven o'clock sharp. And we went up to Spruce Peak where I won the slalom race beating Helmut Schranz ranked twelfth best slalom skier in the world on the FIS point list. I also beat all those important rich white college ski racers. I wore a black logger's hat that made me look like a state trooper out of Mad Magazine.

That's all I have to say about that. Unknown to me was that Connie was my fifth cousin biological some mysterious way. She was such a lovely young lady but already light years too mature for me.

The Great Man Is Here Again

The Great Man Is Here

There was a man who had three wives. He said to the first,

"Go gather the grapes and make wine."

To the second,

"Go pick the peaches and make brandy."

To the third,

"Go pick the corn and make pisco for pisco sours."

So he himself stayed home and boiled some buttons of peyote.

Then a starving woman from Ethiopia found her way up his long driveway and knocked on his door saying,

"You apparently seem to have no wife so marry me?"

So he replied,

"Why would I want to be the father of your starving sons?"

"Because we will know each other and I will gain your valuable knowledge", replied the Ethiopian woman.

Then his wives finally returned to the house after several weeks toiling in the garden,

"Why would you have sex with this starving Ethiopian woman who will bare starving Ethiopian children that we must toil to feed?"

The man scratched his head and said,

"I was horny and wasn't thinking about the consequences, but our earth is abundant here with wild game and wheat and fruit, there is plentiful rainfall to make the crops grow and even fish in the sea. So I perceived that God is good and must have created this planet to feed us all and my faith is great!!"

"Then why don't you run for president?" Added the Ethiopian woman, "Because you are a loving believer and optimist and harbor not negativity, doubt and mistrust."

So the man announced his candidacy and won his political party's support, then won the election because the very good voters turned out at the poll booths.

His nation once again leads the free world and he is speaking again at the United Nations building to the whole assembly,

"I do believe that we can do better, that we are good people and can create a better world for our children. My good people of great faith, my dear supporters I am so inspired by your generosity and benevolence."

"This entire planet benefits from your wisdom and love and is a better place because of your dedication to its environment."

The reporters from The New York Times wrote down his every inspiring word and printed everything he said by nightfall. Everyone went to bed and slept well because the world was at peace now after decades of sheer hell and pandemonium..

Daddy's Gone Away

Daddy you left before I could say goodbye

Daddy's gone away. Should I cry?

I will miss the very grande Norwegian Maple we planted when I was four

I will miss the very large New England Colonial with its leaky roof where I was a child

I will miss the hurricane of 1953 when we cooked everything in the fireplace and ate by candlelight

I will miss the rain that somehow leaked onto my face in spite of the brand new shingles

I will miss high flies in the backyard

I will miss running back into the stone wall and banging my head to catch that deep fly ball you hit

I will miss going to the cemetery to pay respect to your friend who died from the war

I will miss the tall spruce trees I climbed to see the schooners in Long Island Sound

CHAIRLIFT PHILOSOPHER

I will miss the bumpy cobblestone street we lived on and the ride from the train station to pick you up

I will miss Palmer's Market where my mother took me grocery shopping to meet the policeman and the grocery clerk and his sons with girlfriends

I will miss Christmas in New York at your brother's house on Park Avenue with all the holiday lights gleaming in fresh snow

I will miss going with you to Yale Bowl to route for your college team that lost and the long drive home in the dark

I will miss the ski trips way up to Vermont at Mount Snow with your lady friend Mrs. Goodyear and all her children almost my age

We stopped for Swedish Smorgasbord and you always grumbled about the bill but gladly paid it somehow

I will miss the long plane rides to Panama and Lima and Santiago over snowcapped mountains, the Andes

I remember telling you that I would like to live down there

Your reply to me was that I would die, for instance, cougars would have me for dinner

I will miss our few days we skied together in Portillo and I will miss my youth

I will grow old now to be like you and have grandchildren on my knee like you

I will miss my mother who died young. I will miss the runaway dog you let me keep for a friend because I was alone

When you went on long trips all over the world I could not always come along but attended grade school at New Canaan Country Day

I will miss having a second home to go to beside my own, Grandpa's big log cabin with servants and a lanky cigar smoking chauffeur who waxed his car and put gas in it; and all the cheerful kitchen help dressed in rags who had survived Auschwitz death camp

I will miss your sister my Aunt Fran who was always polite and considerate who goaded you over everything like a big sister should

I will miss the horses my cousins rode and all the poop in their stalls I volunteered to shovel

I will miss the chickens that ran into the raspberry and blueberry patches and the hunting dogs that were turned loose to chase the foxes

How we ran behind on foot but not having horses ourselves we missed all the action

So you took me to the car race but a tire came off one car and killed a spectator so we left hurriedly

I will miss that we grew apart when I went off to boarding school but that I loved growing up as it was much more exciting and the world would be mine for a while at least

I will miss that success in this world, at least for me did not last.

I will not miss being sick in midlife crisis with thyroid failure

I will not miss that you disapproved of my divorce even though she filed it against me but told my own children I had deserted them all

I will miss that you forgave me and invited me back into the family on my sixtieth birthday

There I stood at your door ringing the bell as the wet snow soaked my shoes and socks with holes

Then also like you I will not miss this life on Earth entirely because we both know now how terribly disappointing it was

You raced our speed boat out onto Long Island Sound bouncing over the waves like some young naval cadet (plebe) from Annapolis

Because that is what you always were at heart, sailing off into the high seas of adventure

So I reckon that is where you are now on some new voyage beyond the stars

I am a cadet (plebe) too. I followed in your footsteps. I sailed the high seas too

And I will follow you to the stars, Dad. Because you taught me too just as your own dad taught you

My son has come back into my life now here at your funeral he finally approaches me

Now he knows what I know what you knew and Grandpa before you…

I will miss even my cousins who began to hate and tease me, I will forgive them

Just as you have forgiven me, Father…

Our Time Will Come Again

If I am to draw a straight line out from a single point

It cannot go forever but will return to its point of origin

Our one God is at work 24/7

At the end of the long day when you take off your shirt and pull off your socks

Do you not pull them inside out?

God will do this with time in time He will turn it inside out

The Quechua woman in her to phat advises me

"If you go down (from the mats to the city) it is expensive to go down

While There Is Still Time...

If one thing has become increasingly apparent to the people everywhere it is that government by the corporations, for the corporations and of the corporations is now endangering man's existence on earth. Therefore this government based on greed need cease and desist because the planet is bankrupt.

So that all humankind shall rise up to defend itself against this past tyranny of cronyism there need be a new blueprint to insure its demise instead of our own.

The crooks of the Golden Rule have too long been in charge of this our stewardship of this our only planet.

If we are unable to step up to the plate to deter our own destruction by the hands of the few and totally irresponsible then we shall cower and admit we are not stewards at all but a damned race to be replaced by cockroaches and ladybugs.

So therefore the very Green Proletariat must rise from the masses to insure the termination of this industrial revolution which has created this giant catastrophe.

Big Pharma needs to step up and manufacture sufficient doses of happy pills whereby we might all become once again the very happy spear chuckers of the jungles and savannahs.

Our houses need be solar and wind powered so some limited industries need still persist so long as our precious climate is no longer endangered.

Our oceans need be plastic free so such a substance need be outlawed.

We are proposing that this war of the technologically advanced against the ignorant be culminated to the extent where the world's population return to its level before the industrial revolution. So we are looking for volunteers…

Anyone reading this document is to be lined up and shot or sent directly to the nearest Church Supper..…because,

Because it might just be the Last Supper for the human race period.

Inquiries and checks are to be mailed to my address where I have now become a successful hermit until such time when the local food bank runs out because my garden has been destroyed by acid rain and locusts.

Let the reader beware or be wary enough to take some kind of intellectual action now that a degree of intelligence might be required to solve the aforesaid complex pile of insurmountable problems now facing us.

I can be reached at my tropical vacation hideaway where I have gone in denial of this obvious forecast of gloom.

Doomsday is upon us all but probably I, in my tender old age, won't see it So therefore I am leaving all these unsolved problems to you, my sons and daughters. I understand your immense hatred of me because of my incapacity to solve these trying issues in my day.

In your days which are just ahead, likewise most likely your own children shall hate you accordingly and justifiably-

My only regret is that I will not be around to see this justice you now so demand from me unjustly. I inherited this big mess from Granddaddy.

So go in peace and find your own tropical vacation island while there is still time (because the ocean of plastic is fast approaching) amen

Last Summer Read All About It, Extra Extra

FINAL SUMMER

This could be our very last summer so enjoy it! Extra Extra

Gather around my pets and friends. The world is ending, it's just a matter of time.

Now if you eat plastic chicken your world may end even sooner.

It's so very delicious, proclaims my stepmother who ranks ten in sincerity and intent. But in plastic and carcinogen awareness she gets a two

With her in charge of the cooking and buying of foods my father may live to a hundred and nine when he otherwise might live longer than Abraham.

What I am still trying to impress upon you with little luck at all is GREAT HOSPITAL SHIP USA, first in medicine and drugs worldwide! So why are we so far ahead in hospital industry?

We are number one in the world in guinea pigs, among which you and I are included. Yes we are just test animals in THIS GREAT SOCIETY OF CORPORATE WELLNESS, we no longer have rights because these might infringe upon and compromise corporate profits.

So our young men and ladies without trust funds are called upon to serve overseas again in harm's way to be delivered in the GREAT MEAT TRUCK which delivers them to GENERAL HOSPITAL for profit.

Think about it! This is our great American way of life which includes death.

Therefore it is now OUR FINAL SUMMER. So live it up! Extra extra

Read here all about why our stock market is so high and so are all our workers on happy pills quite high also but there shall be an end of all this corporate plundering when you intellectualize which translated means to turn off the television or else continue being brainwashed by it.

Our local newspapers are not much better as BIG PHARM advertises everywhere! We have been bought out by OUR HAPPY PILLS.

So prescribe but sell them all in the streets where our black market economy also is thriving in PILL EXCHANGE. If you don't participate you are in the minority ie less than awesome.

Yes there are polymers released from heating or freezing plastic which is what contains all your food now including plastic lining for your paper(you thought so)coffee cups you drink every morning.

But why should this even matter? Because it's your LAST SUMMER anyway!!

Surprise

For the kingdom of heaven is like a city on a hill and you were young and full of passion when young. It was a hot summer day and you rode down that hill on your bicycle to the sea very easily all downhill because you thought your true love was lying there on the beach in the hot sand near breaking waves and sea gulls. So you went there to play beach ball and volleyball and build sand castles and got all worn out and a bit dehydrated. Instead of drinking water you both needed, you headed over to the bar to drink beer. Now it was over one hundred degrees and your date went off with the bartender to get more beer but didn't return. The sun was going down and quite disappointed as you had become you knew it would be better to bicycle back up the hill from which you had descended. But it seemed very steep so you dismounted and pushed the bicycle which now seemed a burden. You push the bicycle up the cobblestone streets. Some older folks look at you sympathetically. Your date had just been too young and immature but so were you also.

Finally you arrive at the summit as the sun is setting and your father comes out of the house and says,

We didn't know you had even left but the important thing is that you have returned home! There is a big feast for you on the table and all your friends are here, SURPRISE ITS YOUR BIRTHDAY HAPPY BIRTHDAY.

Good thing you came home, huh?

Martyrs For A Green Planet

We will be very fortunate indeed if we can pull off a revolution against big money interests

Probably that will not happen so let us consider

That God is just and good

So if I am to die eventually anyway

Let me have lived for Good cause

That I may be leaning on the road to God

Toward God Himself and not in some other direction

Because my heart is with God

So shall I proclaim myself in His Heart?

Toward the Good for all mankind

Toward man's survival in God's Garden the Earth

And not for selfishness and hedonism like the oil gluttons

Because those who are destroying the planet

For the sake of profit will be held accountable

For high treason against humanity

Let justice begin with their removal from power

Pull them down from their pulpits

Because they are an abomination and hell it is calling them

We need not traitors in our midst-they are an abomination

We will have lived or died in the effort of exposing their corruption

We will have lived that all men might be free from their contamination

We will have lived … truly

And in God's eyes we shall all live forever

In the memory of God that is forevermore and yet a Day

We will all have a place there and that is Heaven itself

Sainthood

Now that you are to become a Saint it's best to let go of the past

There is not much comfort there as reckless youth is universal

All creatures grow and learn by trial and error

Just live by My Commandments and love one another

Treat your very worst enemies as though they are heaven sent saints

Because without Judas to betray Jesus He would not have been crucified and risen

Yes the world is perfect as God intends it in order that you learn some courage and be a hero

Rise up above the doubt and fear and trust in your loving perfect God

Who has placed obstacles and your imagined enemies in your rocky road

Wherefore you yourself are the major obstruction, your own lack of faith!

Perhaps it is because of the sins of your fathers or perhaps it is just the nature of matter in a material world

Which causes you to suffer so but know this that you are not alone

I, the living God, am with you always from the starting post to the finish line I am with thee

Why don't you trust Me and ask Me to relieve your self-inflicted pain

For I will do it, I will remove the heavy yoke upon your shoulders,

I will set you free out of slavery and Egypt! I will bring you to My Promised Land.

Because you treat all others as Saints themselves now it shall be obvious your own Saintliness

Go and walk among your brothers and sisters and confess that it is I, the Lord, who has entered your heart and made you pure

You were just a wretch, a worm of a man, but now you will fly like the butterfly

I have raised you up from the dust in My Image

In order that you see

Booby Trap Nation

Booby Trap Nation

How did this come about, is it no mystery at all?

Or was it done for the profit of the rich and powerful who make the laws

Who govern the Food and Drug Administration?

Come to me all of you who are suckers and see my fluorescent lights

The statue of liberty is now a symbol of great hypocrisy

Everyone comes to America to get higher wages,

To eat our food with so many preservatives

On plastic plates with plastic utensils all microwaved or baked

To release polymers which produce tumors in mice

And turn humans into hospital patients but do not worry,

We have the very best hospitals in the world to care for the sickest people in the world

And luckily for us this is a great business as all our citizens are doctors, lawyers, morticians and soldiers firing ammo

So we will reap dividends eating our hospital meals with plastic disposable forks knives spoons and stir sticks not to forget plastic covers for our plastic plates and our polyester bed sheets

Is there a reason for all this incipient madness and hypocrisy?

Yes! Profit and dividends especially for the lawyers who handle the estates of the deceased and incapacitated.

Do you think I am painting a dismal picture of your country or is it the entire world with its plastic oceans that now has incorporated this philosophy of death?

The Booby Trap Nation beckons you to the New Babylon, a pit in its own self-created hell

Feast and drink the wine with this whore of the earth it has no sex for it is much too unhealthy for reproduction

Then I heard a noise in heaven and it said release the plagues, viruses and locusts to befall this vile nation

At the head of it was the anti-Christ whose head grew a horn like a goat because he had eaten too many pork roasts cooked beneath the earth in a cavern of lust and greed with dribbling fat juices

Many bats flew from their caves and these were now with rabies to bite the heads of those still standing

The seas were full of burning plastic and the great barrier reefs were all dead so every beach was a graveyard of rotting fish in a red tide

And then a man stood up in the U.S. Senate and his name was Bernie and he spoke the truth and everyone laughed at him calling him a forgotten rabbi

Only young babes listened to him their mouths agape in wonderment of the Truth which now was gospel sent from the very seat and throne of the Creator in Heaven, a very distant place

Israel

For some ask me,

"Where is the holy land? Is it Canaan or Samaria or Judah?"

"But I say unto you, look under your own two feet at this your own home or where you might wander,"

"Because I, God, have created you in My own image, so does not an image of your own God dwell upon the earth where you stand?"

"Go and trespass no more in those places where the befallen are drunken and or live in squalor,"

"Because you are My chosen seek a place of refuge, be it a hill or a valley or upon the ocean in a boat, or an island or some continent,"

"Wherever you find rest and tranquility because I, God, am with you and rest My hand upon you there and give you My peace"

"And the name of this sacred place where I shall set you shall be called your new beginning without end"

"Because now the Lord shall be there to dwell among you even in the far ends of the earth, so rejoice!"

For now that you are my servants I shall serve you and wash clean your feet and sustain you and feed you"

"And you shall be My people, you who were oppressed, you who have struggled"

Because now you have overcome, Jacob. so I will call you Israel!"

"Stand vigilant you sons and daughters of Israel for I the Lord am with thee!"

Wide Is The Abyss

For the kingdom of heaven is distant for a man with two happy dogs. He is old and no longer handsome. So he lives alone in the upstairs of the same house with a young couple who live downstairs with a baby. They have a dog as well.

Sometimes all three dogs romp in the yard merrily and sometimes the lady downstairs cooks dinner and sends a plate up to the old man who stares out a window at the sea. The waves are breaking upon the shoreline somewhat craggy with rocks and large stones. Seagulls fly overhead and screech.

The old man once had friends but he wrote a book about them (or at least his personal view of them). This was a terrible disaster and a distortion because as he looked at those friends he could only see one side of them not the far side and so his view was highly subjective depending on his own mood which was affecting their behavior. Of course he wrote down what he saw from his own view but it was ne3ver the whole picture nor was it then exactly the truth.

So he wrote a letter of apology to try and win them back

Dear friends,

I am sorry you did not turn around for me to see the whole picture of you. Perhaps you were hiding something as I often do. So I hereby agree to turn around and face a different direction and find some new friends if you will do the same (I guess you did). Sincerely formerly yours, Me.

The old man sent out the letter from the post office and waited for their replies. One of his former friends wrote back,

Dear old man,

We were all mostly watching your dogs, hoping they were not going to bite us when we finally realized you were the one with the sharp teeth. Go to the dentist and get some smoother gold crowns.

Your former friend,

X

Another former friend wrote:

Dear old man,

I always knew your teeth were sharper than your dogs. They are good company for you as whatever you write about them they do not read your distortions or care one iota so they continue to eat their dog food undisturbed and are happy, sincerely your former friend XX

The old man looked out at the sea where the waves were breaking beneath some distant thunder clouds. He pointed the pistol at his temple and pulled the trigger.

He had forgotten to load the bullets because they were nowhere to be found. The sea gulls cried out their humor to him and he smiled through tears were in his eyes as well as cataracts.

His novel became a best seller and he went on national television but was not permitted to say much. Now he was very famous but lonely.

Marta's House

At Marta's house she was becoming upset by the train of events to come while I never having experienced volcanic eruption first hand well I am of no consolation and have no useful experience. She it's battening down the hatches. The entire sunshine was now blocked out all the windows covered by shutters and our entire rekindled relationship going into the darkness with it. We were forbidden by radio and Television from venturing outdoors. Eventually we lost electricity too as the metal roof was being pelted by sand. It sounded like rain but wasn't. Forty hours later we ventured outdoors into the beach at least it looked like a white sand beach but it was gooey and covered everything. The news on the battery run radio "Bariloche es aislada is isolated" The National Guard would be called out. And owners of four wheel drive vehicles would be asked to truck hay to the starving animals whose grasslands had been covered. Even some ash made it to Buenos Aires Airports closing them down 900 miles away. Wearing a mask I began the very filthy job of cleaning Marta's roofs but I am a roofer and have had filthy jobs before. But I am tracking sand into the house. After eight days of this Marta has had enough. Obviously she says I am not a good person in an emergency and so I must leave tomorrow. I only have $20 I explain but I must leave. Well maybe I can get some wired but obviously I must leave. I leave. I hook all my luggage and ski bag together and drag it down the volcanic sand covered street down to the bus stop where I meet my very good friend the restaurant puppy who shared my fortune my meal and now my misfortune as well as his the volcanic ash-sand covering everything and all my luggage I bid farewell to him and board the bus for the downtown bariloche bus station where I take a bus for Esquel two towns to the south where the volcanic dust has hitherto not been blown by the wind. Esquel is not an overly friendly town though the hostel is clean friendly and relatively unoccupied. So I take many bus rides to the neighboring town traveling and finally that is not adventurous enough so in my search to find skiable snow I board the bus for Corcovado and Carrenleufu.

Under the pursuit of happiness health is our right!.

Epidemic

If there were to be an epidemic in America

Would medical personnel refuse to treat the sick and dying?

There is a national epidemic of corporate greed in America

As we speak our air and water is polluted and the food we eat is full of unnatural chemicals

All of the above have created a national epidemic

Yet the hospitals turn away patients due to overwhelming poverty

If America were well then this poverty wouldn't exist

Now we have become a sick country, luckily there are healthy immigrants flocking to our shores to replace our very sick workforce

Don't they realize there is a corporate epidemic?

We the people have become we the Guinea pigs for experimentation!

People are dying everywhere and it's all for a profit, this is not the pursuit of happiness as defined in our Constitution!

Is there any politician anywhere who will stand up for the people?

Health should be a national right not a privilege of the rich

NATIONAL HEALTH NOW!

We, the American people, deserve to be treated better than "Guinea pigs for experimentation!

Marielle

Marielle Olsen

I had a crush on her some thirteen or fourteen years ago. She was a waitress at the Swiss Chalet in North Woodstock and I could see from the bill that her name on the receptive was waitress: Marielle.

Then I didn't see her again until her spectacular run in the loonatics. Beer League giant slalom in which she placed third in the women's division behind Abby Eaton and Sarah Fast.

She was drinking beer with what appeared to be her brother or a family member. Seems they were keeping a close eye on her as she might drink one too many and go home with whomever her sponsor might be.

Then I realized her last name was Olsen and that she must be of Scandinavian origin like my mother. Still there was no way to approach her.

Yes indeed there was a way into her heart,

"Can I buy you a beer?"

Instantly we became friends even though her seventh sentence would be,

"Well, I'm not going to marry you"

I'm not sure where that came from as I had not proposed anything at all. It became apparent she had a boyfriend or two somewhere at least thirty years younger than me.

Then I met her family at the ski area.

"Marielle had a boyfriend in California who almost beat her to death. She almost died. She was in the hospital a month."

Her mother confided this to me.

"Well my mother was half Swedish. "I replied, "So maybe we are distant cousins?"

Wrong line. I was supposed to say,

"My daddy is very rich and I am in the family business over twenty years now and am interested in your beloved daughter and can take care of her!"

Point lost. She has a new boyfriend but he is a fish in Bethlehem.

So I visited her, them, at norm Desjardins in Bethlehem where I determined him to be a barefooted hippy painter with a gallon of tequila.

"Marielle likes soccer," he said and kicked the ball past her. They both chased it. Since I was wearing shoes I kicked it much too far.

Not sure how I tricked her into my car, perhaps because he didn't have one. in any case we were heading to lobster night in the basement restaurant of Thayer's Inn. Marielle had a Tequila Sunrise followed by a Sonora Sunset or something. Plus a lobster she didn't finish. A bad sign.

It became quite late as sipping these concoctions at the bar and chatting with my friend Rob took endless hours until the bartender announced,

"We are closing now!"

So Marielle came to my house and met the dogs both friendly and eager.

"You can sleep on the couch, "I insisted not wanting to face her mother if something more intricate happened under the influence of alcohol.

"I want to sleep in a bed!" She suggested.

"Mine is full of dogs, you'll be happier on the couch "I later regretted.

I woke up at my usual six o'clock and took the dogs to McDonald's for my coffee and there sausage biscuits.

Marielle slept peacefully until noon and then was ready for a game of chess I had promised. She made some very surprising moves. In any case I lost.

"You are much smarter than you act sometimes, "I observed.

"Yes I went to college," she replied.

She even graduated and was on the ski team at St Michaels in Burlington.

"Oh I know where that is." at least I knew of it.

Marielle survived chess and lobster and returned to her steaming mad boyfriend who wanted to fight with her. She ditched him.

Within a week she had a new boyfriend also a barefoot hippy but this new one was a carpenter. He had a big Bowie Knife but he used it more for Satanic Ceremonies than throwing at trees like Vietnam vets do.

I went to visit her at her mother's house where she took care of her aging father with dementia. The new boyfriend had immediately moved in there to assist her and the mother thought all this was splendid as she escaped each weekend to her job bus tours to New York, Washington and Philadelphia.

I brought Marielle some extra boots and race skis as the new race season was approaching. I vacationed in Denmark and sent her pictures of the Little Mermaid Statue in the North Sea Harbor dedicated to Hans Christian Andersson's famous children's stories.

Her boyfriend got a job at maintenance at Indian Head Motel but must have been fired because he was soon working nearby as a maid. His great success enabled him to bring home a daily gallon of vodka and Marielle insisted into the night to drink most of it. They were soon fighting and she had a big lump on her cheek as well as a swollen forehead with headaches.

"Marielle, you don't look so well, maybe you should go to the Hospital?" I asked.

"I fell through some missing boards on my porch to the deck below. John (the name of all her boyfriend had been John), John took me to the Hospital in Littleton."

"Well that's good," I inquired, "Did they find any broken bones?"

"Maybe my ribs are broken" she replied then lied,

"It was my father who hit me in the forehead!"

I went skiing in South America for a few weeks and when I returned the news was pretty much the same.

"I'll sponsor you at loonatics pay for your $28 lift ticket since you don't have a job still and no money"

"John doesn't like it when I ski" she replied.

"You are a ski racer, Marielle it's your thing you do best! Be happy, "I pleaded.

Marielle missed most of the races this last winter. She didn't like slaloms anyway, preferred the wider open giant slaloms. Though I sponsored her we never managed to take one run together.

I had gone out west spring skiing and while I was gone my ski racing friend Billy Crampton from Tenney Mountain suffered a severe stroke, lost the ability to eat and to talk. But on his Facebook page I noticed he said,

"So tragic we have lost another one of our talented ski racing friends, Marielle Olsen."

It appears evident she went missing in the Pemigewasset River just a week ago after being seen near Lady's Bath a swirling basin upriver from her home.

Her friends searched for her several hours then called police who sent a diving unit into Lady's Bath next morning with no results. A few hours later by then the afternoon some friends spotted her body downriver a few miles and called the police.

Rest in Peace, Marielle, you are not on the mountains or in the townships but have travelled on the stars.

Ski Racer

For the kingdom of heaven is like a young ski racer going up the Santiago ski lift with his young wife. He says to her,

"Look at all these pine trees and some with blight, I don't like them because it means it doesn't snow much here. I would rather ski among the spruce trees!"

"What is wrong with you?" she protests and divorces him a year later.

"Forty years go by and the ski racer is now old going up the Santiago ski lift with a slightly younger fiancé.

"Look at these lovely pine trees. They are so healthy and happy!"

"Yes they are so lovely and so pretty, she smiles and agrees.

A year later they marry and live happily ever after because he has a change of heart. It did not happen overnight. It is though he has been born again or reborn in a new happy kingdom.

Abandoned

I recall I suffered the flu and had been vomiting and had almost no heat supply in my house other than wood which I had not gathered in sufficiency. At any rate I felt very sick and with a fever of over one hundred I checked into the only pet friendly motel in South Fork, Colorado with my main father dog of all my dogs, JP, and a very sick puppy I did no longer want to see suffer in the cold as he was terminally ill. However JP's sister Sara of whom I was most fond because she was a darling too, I had to leave at my freezing cold uninsulated house in Alpine Village, a remote subdivision on the outskirts of town going toward Del Norte. She had just had a litter of puppies in my Ford F'150 pickup and I had just given them each a half booster of puppy parvovirus and distemper vaccines. So I left poor Sara at the house with a very large bag of dog food there and noticed her look of disapproval but I promised her I would return next dawn and left for the motel in a heavy snowstorm while she busily was breastfeeding the entire litter.

Unfortunately my fever became steadily worse through the night and I was too sick to even go for coffee or out the door next morning and my small sick one year old, Houdini, did not pass the night well either. The wind picked up and howled and the snowstorm became a blizzard. I prayed for the safety of my dog pack but to no avail.

A nosey female neighbor with a drug addiction problem in her past and symptoms of bipolar disorder who had handed out towels at the Glenwood

Springs swimming pool and received for a tip snorts of cocaine, well she had befriended the local veterinarian in Del Norte. She noticed my dogs at my house across the street so snooped on over to see their water dish had frozen which constituted animal cruelty of some kind in her mind so she gathered all the puppies and Sara and took them to her friend the veterinarian. I never saw Sara again or those pups who were all taken to City Market in Alamosa the next day and given away in the parking lot at the vet's suggestion.

Life being cruel and even more so in the high remote Rocky Mountains, my one year old Houdini barked at a Mexican who had backed up into my car at a different motel in Monte Vista a whole month later. My poor little dog had laid there with no breath at all on a warm blanket with his rare fungus lung disease he had contracted from water that drips from the leaves of deciduous trees in Alabama or Louisiana but somehow that fungus had spread to New Hampshire because of global warming the previous summer. Of course the Sheriff in Twin Mountain had decided that my five dogs constituted a threat to my blond haired female neighbor with very big teats who he had the hots for. So me and my dogs felt very unwelcome by his constant visits as he was just another bad cop that took bribes and was looking for one from me, we left town instead.

Some flying saucers which I hadn't noticed but which the dogs had begun barking at moving around strangely in the sky overhead seemed to be trying to warn the dogs of imminent danger being the State Police and a Sergeant Koler who had become the state of New Hampshire's leading expert on psychoanalysis, so he claimed on routine traffic stops. My F 150 Ford got impounded by him and towed off to his brothers garage, nepotism is it called?

All the dogs and me headed out west but Macayla decided to run away in the Walmart parking lot in Canon City when we arrived in Colorado. I guess she got tired of so many endless hours of driving across country. Perhaps it is true I was not the best dog owner as I too was suffering from undiagnosed slow thyroid.

My ex-wife's doctor recommended that I start radiation treatments for thyroid cancer. I left both her and that doctor in Avon thinking maybe they were in cahoots.

Life is so cruel. Spotted Scotty got separated from the pack in Missouri and Oscar Mayer had failed to clear a barb wire fence in South fork chasing his father JP who was chasing something. Small children found Oscar tangled in barb wire and their father took him to the vet who recommended he be put down as his leg not savable. But I had sold some parcel of land and had money for the operation and so he became a three legged dog only to disappear in Illinois a year later.

Now this brings me back to life being cruel and I heard from Dusty Fullenwider, the real estate lady that a dog was loose in

Alpine Village that looked like one of my breed, Sara and JP had come from a litter of my neighbor Everett. Now Everett was missing all his toes because falling down drunk in winter his feet had frozen and to save his life all his gang green toes had to be amputated. He had even drugged me at his house in my coffee in the hope of raping me but he admitted next day when I woke up that I had been to, tough and uncooperative with his efforts so I was not his type after all. Nice neighbor!

So anyway I had driven my F'150 and JP to the far reaches of Alpine Slopes number seven subdivision and there running skittish between some abandoned summer cabins was a familiar looking dog, definitely a son of JP. The crazy bitch neighbor of mine on cocaine had missed one and it went wild and survived on that big bag of dog food left there and now it was a year old perhaps. I coaxed it over to the truck with bits of food then took it for a ride with JP but it was too wild and growled then fought with JP its father. It had become a ravenous wolf. I had to let it out of the truck and never saw it again but was reassured some unknown neighbor was still feeding it.

Eventually I was taken away in an ambulance to a hospital with barred windows where two young genius doctors agreed I had failed thyroid and just needed to take a small pill daily. I got my dog JP back and my life improved steadily even though JP got old and died. It was very heartbreaking and he and his family and I had been through so much together. Now finally I had lost them all but my godson who moved in with me found a couple of Rottweiler pups at McDonald's. It turned out their mother had bitten the mailman in Dalton, NH and so the town sheriff there went over and confiscated her to the firing squad.

I had been adopted by rich folks when just a baby and they told me my racial ethnicity was starving Armenia. Then they fought, divorced and separated. She went to an asylum. I went ski racing up on high mountain sides to escape life's constant cruelty.

So at one ski race when a blonde chubby woman with a lot of mascara approached me years back way long ago and said she was my mother I thought perhaps she was playing a practical joke on me. I jumped on the ski lift and went back up the mountainside and never saw my birth mother again. How tragic.

I guess I was like that one wild dog abandoned in that blizzard, now I was running free and such a wolf there would be no further effort at domestication. And my birth mother was like the driver of a pickup Ford F 150 she had been sick with morning sickness and quarreling with her husband my birth father down there in Alabama and had runaway back to her aunt Doris who was also a beauty there living with her grandparents the Hortons in Brockton, Massachusetts.

Now I have to apologize to my uncle Charles her brother whom I expect to meet at my race at Okemo ski resort, Vermont tomorrow. I have raced there since 1961 and I am now seventy years old and he is seventy six being the youngest by far of his siblings.

Life is quite a tragedy unfolding and I am not fully aware yet why we must suffer so and or why dogs who are the most loving obedient creatures must suffer with us. Surely they don't deserve it. I think I won so many medals skiing in my long career just to distract me from so many unpleasantries and disappointments. The young lady I loved the most as a young ski champion died before her time of brain cancer and tried to reach me by telephone one last time, we had been separated by parents and destiny and schools apart and time. She called but I didn't have a telephone.

My own mother must have thought I was like a rabid dog or a wild sled dog gone to live in the Call of the Wild. I did. I am still up there on that high mountain. Maybe we will all be there across that great chasm that great stream when we all die we shall cross to the other side and see the ones we miss so dearly, taken from us by this cruel cruel world but then we shall reunite and be altogether One again. I hope so. I sure miss you all!

Arlene

My birth mother had been Arlene Anderson Perry. She had been married to my birth father in Alabama after the Second World War which had defeated those maniachel Germans, Japanese and Italians. She had been held captive at home there in Alabama where women were not yet liberated against her liberal Massachusetts will and had managed to escape on the bus back to her aunt Doris in Easton, Massachusetts very close to Brockton. Aunt Doris had just married a Chase for mostly good name and financial security, and she suggested to Arlene that she better find a career and give up on the idea of raising a child without a husband to support her.

So my mother gave me up for adoption for ten thousand dollars to a nice well to do couple in Weymouth, the husband of which was a Lieutenant in the U.S. Navy. And Arlene signed up with the Woman's Air Force (WAF) and served in the Korean War in Japan shortly thereafter. She was basically a cocktail waitress in an Officers Lounge and met some high brass. This landed her a job as a receptionist for Sikorsky helicopters in the mid 1950's shortly thereafter where she met an interesting fellow with a German accent, Mr. Baxter from Argentina. He had a wife probably somewhere and some daughters and a niece or some such from his relatives in California named Hodie. Possibly Hodie Hazard???Obviously they were all Germans displaced by the War. Mr. Hazard seemed attractive enough but was sort of crazy. It turned out a nice Jewish man named Kissinger had recruited him to fly as a spy for us in the Korean war and he had been shot down and wounded in the head and had a plate there on the side of his skull. He had some behavior problems and had been in an Irish Pub in New York City where he was mistaken after several beers of being a former Nazi officer so they beat him up severely and broke his one good leg, the other leg being a peg leg because it had been amputated in perhaps December 1944 in a bombing raid over Germany but then this turned out to be incorrect as he later admitted flying a plane in the Luftwaffe that was shot down by Russian ground forces near Berlin. And he just so happened to know the man who had adopted her son, me. Small world!

Arlene was of course a blonde which had attracted the German pilot, now some sort of technical advisor working for Sikorsky. Her paternal grandparents had emigrated from Motala, Sweden in the latter eighteen hundreds and been recruited brought to America in part by Ames Shovel Company of Easton, Massachusetts which explains at least in part how her family ended up there, the Andersons who I later in life hunted down to get their story but by that time of course Arlene was deceased as she had gotten that awful cancer and died in 1983 at age fifty four down where she had moved to work in a hospital in Providence, Rhode Island.

Your Blanket

He is like the messiah

Who stands before his God ashamed of his nakedness

And begs forgiveness for his innumerable sins

*Oh my God I humbly ask Your pardon

For my transgressions which are numbered like grains of sand

For the spew that comes out of my mouth like spit

For all my uncleanliness and my evil thoughts

Raise me up oh God and make me whole

For I am partial, just a worm of a man

I long to fly like a butterfly

Give some beauty to my life, let me love

Let me love all Your laws

Written for my protection

But give me love and compassion too

Let me forgive those who trespass against me

And let them forgive me also

I am but a man on a path

I did run out of Egypt

For I have been a slave of temptation

Deliver me from evil

Give me Your commandments, let me obey

Raise me up onto Your holy mountain

Yes bring me to the promised land of milk and honey

And make an everlasting covenant with me

Like a blanket to cover my nakedness and shame

In order to warm me on cold, dark and lonely nights

Let me sleep forever with You

And find rest and peace, amen

The Garden

The Garden

The pollution in my city

Is of such an extent

That my brothers, sisters and cousins

Are dying well before their time

From pollution of air and water

From backed up gases in the sewer

From the aromas of asphalt

From synthetic clothing derived from oil.

I see it in the faces of the people

Commuting on the Transmilenio'

It didn't used to be THIS WAY

Colombia was a Garden of Eden

Then came the ambition of lazy men

Who decided to no longer toil on the farm

They decided to become the managers of other men and businessmen

They decided for the easy life on Easy Street

Riding around in luxury cars smoking cigars

Chasing their counterparts' whores disguised as secretaries.

Heart attack, cancer, emphysema and aids ensued.

Now we have all these great castles of the rich

Condominiums

But the quality of life has not improved one iota,

In fact it has plummeted

And the stock market with it,

Up and down, up and down, all this confusion

Is so stressful.

The Rose once bright and aromatic

Is now wilted beyond recuperation

So it is time to plant a new crop of leaders in our assemblies of government

CHAIRLIFT PHILOSOPHER

Who will bring the necessary change

So that the sky of all this smog will clear

That the sun may shine once again!

And the people will smile and be happy

Kingdom

The kingdom of heaven is like when a man leaves his native land after graduating school to find work in a distant land and success there. He is thrilled, happy and exuberant and he is not sure he wants to go back to his native country as it was a land of no or less opportunity. So it will be when you find yourself reborn into a covenant with God, you don't look back into Sodom and Gomorrah in your rear view mirror because you would see flames licking your rear license plate.

The kingdom of heaven is like a young man on a bicycle fresh out of school he travels down the highway and everywhere he goes people are amazed he has come so far just by pedaling. He sleeps behind churches or in cornfields because it is now warm summer weather which is great for bicycling.

'Thank you God,' he says for providing me with this amazing bicycle with its good light wheels, smooth bearings and a well-designed derailleur'

As long as he is so thankful he is full of great joy and will continue to have a wonderful trip. Woe to him who is unthankful for he enters nearest to the gates of hell itself and is pursued by demons, robbers and the unclean. Better he should stop whatever he is doing and go home quickly to lie under heavy bed covers and blankets...

For the kingdom of heaven is like a huge celebration on a national Indepence Day when many young people become drunk or even take drugs to watch fireworks thinking in vain, willfully imagining that they are free spirits when actually they are being pursued by many demons so now they are mentally ill because they are now slaves to their many indulgences sex, drugs, alcohol and loud music. While many more mature adults observe them and recollect how they themselves were once young and foolish now they feel independent of all that pain and suffering such as carnal love-it is because they asked God for help only He could provide them. So He intervened and gave them peace in a new life in Him

Boy From Ipanema

"We are going to borrow someone else's kid when we have dinner with the president of Brazil, and we will leave you on the beach in your own room to do whatever you please," said my father.

My father had brought me with him to Cuzco, Peru where we walked up a long hot dry hill almost breathlessly to a Cathedral where he knocked on the door and inquired about the presence of a certain monk.

"Oh no, he's no longer here!" insisted the priest angrily while trying to close the door on my father's invading shoe polished very well like they do that in the Navy.

Evidently we were inquiring about a monk rumored to be Martin Bormann, Hitler's adjutant general. He had fled that monastery at the request of the U.S. State Department for more fatchist friendly Asuncion, Paraguay only to catch Yellow Fever and die there. Another rumor perhaps that one is.

Yet now on Ipanema where I had a very cheap motel room that was the best one offered, I waved goodbye not terribly affectionately as I had been ditched for the presidential dinner where I might spill the beans about my father's being a U.S. Agent not a tobacco tsar like his brothers in Connecticut.

The Brazilian girls on the beach informed me that their boyfriends were coming after dark to kill me if they would find me with them. So I took their advice and wandered into the suburbs to attend all night drinking parties at several big rich mansions as it goes on like that in Rio De Janeiro nightly.

Meanwhile my father and stepmother, Dorothy, attended an extravagant state sponsored dinner with the newly elected leftist Brazilian president whose child entertained my father's replacement child with my name surely. They wandered freely in the compound those children playing games etcetera. From my impostor replacement and his memory of that evening were drawn detailed maps of the entire compound for the right wing junta that toppled the government one year later.

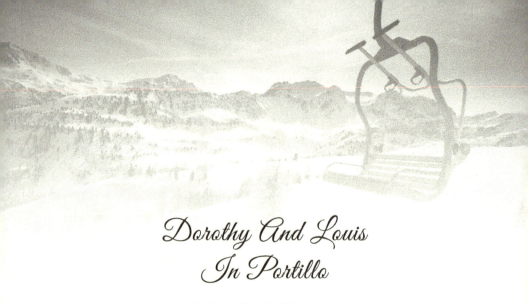

Dorothy And Louis In Portillo

My father had divorced my convalescent mother Thais, the papers being filed by her in 1956. So he had several girlfriends including the estranged Mrs. Goodyear whose children enjoyed all our combined family ski vacations at Bromley in Vermont where we stayed with John Luannetti and his wife at their bed and breakfast The South Londonderry Inn. These were among the most enjoyable years of my life because on ski weekends I suddenly had a family was a member of a big pretend family. with sisters and a brother almost but Mrs. Goodyear never did take kindly to me.

Then there was Mrs. Roper another divorcee but she had no kids and did not ski. But drink like a fish she did the wine mostly red and expensive. But I broke through a barricade hearing my father's crying to see that she in fact was a man maybe. I told the kid with brains at school Matty Matthews who told his parents and Mrs. Roper was arrested for drunken driving and they found a dildo in her purse. So the Republicans won that election not Mrs. Roper.

Then along came Dorothy who abstained from alcohol and my father had always known and liked her and she him… when her husband died and she wore a black veil for a few weeks.

She liked Vermont so ski trips were back on the agenda and no dildos to my knowledge. She preferred more her blindfolds so she could pretend she was still with the original husband perhaps or who knows. My father had a gun in his drawer by the bed upstairs. I think it was a browning semi-automatic but I never touched it or opened the book beneath it which was entitled Der Bund or Bundes league or somesuch, it was in German I finally did open it once. It had names of officers and meeting places perhaps where Yale students could show support for American Isolationism.

My father many years later when I confessed to him having had dinner in Bariloche with Lipski and his daughters or were they daughters of his second wife maybe one was.

"Lipski was a great man!" said my father.

I don't want to hold him to this as an incriminating remark as maybe he just was trying to impress me by knowing of everybody I knew… but of course history points out in endless textbooks that Lipski, the Polish Ambassador to Berlin in the 1930's was a close friend to Hermann Goring, Reichmarshall of all Prussia and Luftwaffe flying ace of World War I. Lipski mapped for Goering locations and sizes of all Jewish settlements in Poland and locations of synagogues even though Lipski was in fact Jewish

In Bariloche where Lipski was sent by the Nazis in September 1939 as Poland ceased to exist after its invasion he wore a big round Jewish Rabbi hat and though I didn't inspect it personally I was told it was pure mink or several of them their furs interwoven. Lipski was a lawyer and in Argentina passed the bar and prepared legal documentation for the Germans of high rank should they lose the war, almost unthinkable but it proves someone was thinking somewhere in that Third Reich.

Lipski had asked me who the survivors of the Warsaw Ghetto Uprising had surrendered to and I had thought probably the Russians, He corrected me but in my disbelief as it seemed unlikely they had surrendered to the Germans in exchange for German citizenry-well I was 16 did not know all my history but was asked to leave before the meal. I left, his wife and daughters apologized. I had met one on the ski slopes there Argentina.

That was all 1964 but I have to return to the year before this 1963 when Lewis and I went to Portillo Chile to ski for two weeks and out of the clear blue sky Dorothy arrived. We all set at our nice table with its tablecloth bread and wine. I think it was spaghetti in white sauce. Over in the less lit corner set the tall blonde haired man slightly bald, yes that German again from out of the clear blue sky with his family the English wife he met when he befriended the English pilot Douglas Bader after the war. The two blond daughters were there also now twelve or thirteen years old perhaps. They had been five and six when I had met them all in Pound Ridge, New York at their Dutch colonial house with the red fence, Golden Retrievers and of course the pond with rowboat.

Rudel, that tall man's name, he was getting noisy and drunk by the minute talking with the family ski instructor Dixie Nohl an Austrian. He was making some loud insults in German but then in English aimed at our table and my father who he apparently still did not like. Next thing I know he comes walking over to our table alone standing there drunk and loud proclaiming to my father,

"You were never a soldier! You were never on the frontlines! You were never in any war-so you cannot possibly know anything at all!"

"I was a weatherman in Morocco and our field was strafed by Messerschmits firing fifty caliber rounds. Three of us were killed on the base, yes that was my only experience…"

"You can't even fight "said Rudel mockingly.

I was only fifteen years old but I had been in a lot of fights every recess at school and I could not stand this man insulting my father so I jumped up and clenching my fists I said to that Nazi pilot,

"I'll fight you, I am not afraid!"

Dorothy yelled at me like a sleeping lioness now awakened,

"Sit back down, immediately!"

I did.

Chanukah Poem

Please God forgive a sinner like me

And bring me to the free box of Your eternal grace

Have mercy like a treasure chest

To bestow on me and mine

Your glad tidings of Chanukah.

Rescue me from my enemy

The evil one who has corrupted the earth with money for avarice

If you have little of it that is a blessing to protect you

From your fallen self in the muck and mire.

Raise me up oh lord from the pigsty of sin

To clean mountain water

A clear stream of righteousness.

I want to dwell with You most high

Let me be free and soar like an eagle,

Like a condor above the eternal snows

For Your love is constant and innumerous

As the snowflakes and raindrops that fall from heaven

To relieve the earthly drought and suffering and hunger.

Make my heart pure and snow white like lamb's wool

Provide a cloak for me on this my day of suffering

Because I am not with You

I am still less than an angel

But soon because of Thy steadfast Love

I will soar above the earth liberated and free

Of the chains of sin and death

Because You alone are my Liberator

You have brought me out of Egypt

Into the Promised Land

Slow Freddy

There was a young man named Freddy in awe of the holy spirit who was agape more or less and he ran around with his mouth wide open as though he were in awe of something unseen invisible but he seemed to see it.

One day he met a young woman named Francine whose lower jaw did hang very low. At one time doctors tried to wire her jaw shut but the result was a total failure and her mouth was always wide open except for when she sipped through a straw.

The two seemed destined for each other and at midnight mass or afternoon mass they always sat together in the first row of pews in the great Cathedral of St Mary with their mouths wide open as if beholding angels.

A full nurse once told both of them that people whose mouths are always open were generally proved to be of lesser intelligence. The nurse would go around the city and point out persons of lesser intelligence whose mouths were wide open.

Now then came an extreme famine in the land and everyone was starving. Freddy and Francine were going door to door begging for food and they looked starving with their mouths wide open and people fed them what they could.

Then the nurse came door to door with her mouth closed tight shut and the homeowners offered her no food at all because she was a high nurse and thought everyone in the town was an idiot. Unfortunately she starved to death and no one felt sorry for her at all.

The moral of the story is that it is permissible to act stupid in public as long as you can do it gracefully because if you are clever and smart but have not grace no one is going to enjoy your clever wit anyway.

We Follow Jesus In Our Procession

We follow Jesus in our procession

We follow Jesus with His cross

On foot on bicycle on skates on horse (but not in cars alone)

Through clouds of smog and doubt

Because His Words of Faith are the Way are the Path

We had lost our faith we had lost our way and stumbled

Our bride had been taken from us

We were robbed by false doctrines, by false practitioners

Who took our money but could not cure us

There is only One Healer, One Doctor for our ills

He is followed by one thousand umbrellas in a tearful procession

Through raindrops of our weeping

About the destruction of our environment

Our mother the planet

"Come back to your mother you lost people!"

We were conquered and sent it the captivity of despair

For our sins but we now repent

Of our lust and greed, we had lost our way in darkness

But now our Nation shall be restored to us

He will place us once again on our Holy Hill Jerusalem in Zion

Because hope is now lifted up within us

"Go and sin no more, pollute no more nor sit in laziness"

"But rise up and breath and Walk as He does!"

Now the sunshine shall be returned to us

Let us be jubilant and joyous

Now that Eden is restored, Our Garden Eternal!

We had families before but now we have only Jesus Our Saviour

I have seen Him, He is risen

He is there in Chia we have seen him

CHAIRLIFT PHILOSOPHER

He is there and everywhere

Now He liberates our conquered City

Now he sets us captives free

Find Him and live forevermore

Study The Book Of Life Like A Hebrew Even If You Are Not One, Just Imagine You Could Be

No Abraham no family,

Know Abraham know family.

No Job no faith,

Know Job have faith.

No Elisha no hope,

Know Elisha know hope.

No Moses no law,

Know Moses know justice.

No David no shame,

Know David know repentance,

CHAIRLIFT PHILOSOPHER

No Solomon no glory

Know Solomon know splendor.

No Jesus no grace

Know Jesus know peace.

No God no love,

Know God feel the love.

Pornography destroys but Jesus heals

So study diligently the words spoken in the book of life,

Be wiser and spread your wings like an eagle

Let your mind behold your Creator.

Othmar

Othmar Schneider, the guatleitler of Portillo Province guided us all across the barely frozen lake in the high Andes and up into a saddle at thirteen thousand feet where he gave us his farewell speech.

"Now all of you have been under my jurisdiction for quite a few years and I wish you all well. I have tried best to guide you to achieve success in the world as you I regard were under my responsibility and I have tried my very best. You are going on to greater things while I am going into maybe another job or two before my retirement…"

So it is with you are younger than me and still fail to understand my motives: I will be held accountable for not guiding you to a better future, if I am to suggest nothing and say nothing this will be viewed by my God as gross negligence on my part and I will be thrown into Hades for foolishness.

So listen to what I say because it is not just some trip I am on in vacationland: it is my real true experience and I am not lying to you or my value will decrease in the eyes of the Almighty.

These changing times require action and I have not been able to accomplish very much but with your understanding and obedience to the task at hand we might still accomplish a great workman amazing production

Gautleiters were overseers in Austria and Germany so each South American German population had one overseer as well.

My last day in Bariloche on the seventy gate slalom hill I was summoned over to "Otto" whose last name was Zucchini or Scarzini, something Italian I thought.

His men laughed as I said the word "Italian".

"Someday you will figure it out, Kuhlmann!"

"We have our own heroes in North America, we don't study German history in high school," I replied.

"In any case you cannot come back here to Argentina, Kuhlmann" said Skorzeny.

He implied that times were changing and that not even the ex-nazis would still be welcome there. Unknown to me he just purchased a home in Ireland.

"Any other questions?" he asked me.

"Yes, well is that pilot my father?" they all observed me.

"No, Kulmann, I am your father!" replied Otto.

"Oh, I thought so, I agreed. They all laughed at the notion that he was my father. He was theirs as well now, I thought.

"Goodbye, Kuhlmann!" he retorted almost teary eyed.

"Oh, Otto" his men chuckled.

I skied down to Club Andino to pack my bags and waited for my taxi apprehensively because a small man with a mustache came out of the kitchen with a medical bag to give me a shot for the flu.

"I feel better now and don't need a shot!" I insisted.

"Just how would you fight me if you had to?" Inquired the small man, Doctor Fritz (Mengele, the Death Angel of Auschwitz Extermination Camp)

"I would kick you with my feet!" I exclaimed.

"Oh, you are a Frenchman!" exclaimed Mengele.

We had a twenty five minute conversation during which he put backfiring dueling pistols on the table and challenged me to shoot him.

"Why would I want to do that?" I cowered, "You are my mentor!" I would brown nose him to save my life.

He began having an argument with the Hostel manager who told him that I was such a good guy to be leaving him my dirty ski parka. Mengele insisted that the parka would be his own.

The taxi arrived and took me to Marta's Slovenian grandmother who had been instructed to bring me to the central Hospital for a flu shot. This was standard procedure for handling unwelcome snoopy foreigners.

"I'll tell them you are feeling better and don't need a shot, stay in the car," she insisted.

Then we went to her hotel where I was given room number twenty with no windows but a dresser to barricade the door. At midnight they came to my door.

"Bala Perdida, come out and play!" cried the voices. I played dead.

The next morning at six the cab came for me to take me to the airport. I had spent an entire month in jail for supposedly threatening the peace but it had been a setup.

I was very happy eating a cheeseburger in Miami Airport. I was home at last.

The Duke

The Duke was born back in 1933 in a coal mining town just north of Paonia, Colorado. This made him a witness to the great generation that had served their country in the Second World War and so he stepped up to the plate and enlisted for service in the Korean Conflict which was actually a full scale war with as many or more Aussies, Canadians and Kiwis dying in combat as in World War Two.

So the Duke whose real name I can't quite recall heard the order given not to fire at a Russian Mig which would soon strafe their position. American troops were being killed and the Duke opened up with his Tommy gun spraying the cockpit of the low flying aircraft which he helped bring down onto an airfield perhaps within two miles.

The pilot was none other than Hans Ulrich Rudel, a WWII flying ace from the Third Reich who at the bequest of henry Kissinger had gone back home to what became Communist East Germany which of course drafted its talent in support of North Korea and China. His mission as a spy had been to locate any possible survivors of the Wehrmacht that had surrendered to Stalin thereupon were marched through Moscow in chains and shipped to Siberia to die.

Stalin had been successful and Rudel himself had not as bullets entering the cockpit of his plane creased his skull and he put his finger upon the hole to keep his brains from running out, although some were already in his lap he managed a shaky landing behind American lines.

The Duke was court marshalled but exonerated later after his military discharge.

Of course Rudel soon went to work for Sikorsky in Connecticut. His son would coach the U.S. Ski Team under an alias.

I loved his son's stories and lecturing to mostly the U.S. Women's ski team. I had read widely as even a youth and been exposed to Nietzsche and the son, my elder by several years, had attended a prominent New England College and was very well educated which I was not. I did remember a previous time when he the son had confessed the famous Nazi pilot was his father but then pointing a Luger at me demanded I take a memory loss pill as he had told me too much and that I must forget.

Then his father had done the same when I went for a ride in his pointless stainless steel 1953 Porsche shipped from West Germany to Argentina. You guessed it, I won a ski race in Argentina which I had been ordered not to win because of a very large Calcutta and some Argentine general had bought me as a long shot then won big. My German sponsors were furious and thought my skis I had bought from Jean Claude Killy in Portillo contained some magical device enabling me to ski through a flush all dirt as I ran dead last and all snow there being absent I still had won the race trofeo Vanoni.

So Rudel had blindfolded me at gunpoint and taken me to Llao-Llao where there was a basement jail cell for the disorderly. I had been knocked out by a luger blow to my shoulder. I woke up my eyes taped open my hands cuffed behind me and I watched the Nuremberg Rally featuring of course the Fuhrer Adolf Hitler and his many followers into Hell itself. But I would forget most of this by the time I returned to the States where my father and stepmother thought best to commit me to the Looney Bin!

Eventually I would be let out of there to ski in the junior Nationals and win under the guidance of coach Paul Kailey of Gould Academy one of the very few decent ski coaches I have ever met and from my successes I took my spot on the U.S. Ski Team for well over a year but I was by their standards much too wild a child.

In Argentina they had tried to brainwash because the communist North Koreans and Chinese had forged an early lead in this field. I believe they had told me to go to Siverthorne, Colorado and look for a guy named Duke and kill him: that was my mission and it was to fulfill Rudel's revenge over his brains spilling out and the plate in his head.

Of course I finally did meet the Duke who quite possibly had been told that I did have a secret message for him or worse. But the Duke and his two boys were my friends as we drove around Nucla and Naurita together even to Delta and Montrose. The West never quite catch up to those Manchurians in brainwashing!

Listen To The Word Of God That He Is Good

O mortal man, why do you hate?

It profits you nothing to hate your mortal destiny, you shall die regardless

Your loving God allows you to return to the dust from which you came,

From which you grew up to be vibrant and full of joy that you live

Even more so should you rejoice in your immortal body

Because God might reward you with eternal life through him

If you shall believe in love, his love that he died for your sins upon that cross

In order to prepare for you a place where he has gone you might be also

Though you must believe in love that it comes from God and may enter you

To destroy all hatred and fear forever, they are the same as doubt and death

So rise up from defeat and destruction, rebuild your city from its ashes

Rebuild the walls inside your heart and so love everyone and every small thing

Because the loud shall soon cry and the very silent shall utter the truth

So when he speaks to you, listen to the word of God that He alone is good

O mortal man rejoice in God's perfect plan to remove you from mortality

To give you immortality through Him, He comes for you with His Sacred Heart

How he loves you that you might understand through His Grace

That you shall be most graceful as well and appreciative of every small thing

Of every small child and every puppy and each tiny kitten let joy fill your heart

Do not kill, do not steal, and do not lie with another man's wife

Do not divorce, do not envy and do not doubt that God loves us all

So the arrogant man points a gun at his own head, do not envy him

Walk softly and be gentle like a summer breeze from offshore

The new time is coming when you shall behold your God, yes you shall see Him

He might even appear to you in the mirror if you shall love yourself by loving others

They are each one of them struggling for his or her freedom from bondage in Egypt

We were all slaves to sin which trapped us in most unfavorable circumstances

Therefore we were arrested for our own good, we were booked into the jail cell

We had so threatened our own safety that we were led into captivity

O immortal God please deliver us back home where we belong with friends and family

Our children and pets miss us so and long for our return

Let us greet them all with open arms and open hearts and speak the truth

That God saves us always and has never failed to do so

Never failed to do so, never never and will always rescue us forever

Why didn't you believe this your entire life? Why did you doubt the truth?

Because you lied you became lost you would not admit your errors and sins

Confess them now to God, my dear God I do confess that I have been tempted by darkness

I do confess that I am lost because I was led in a wrong direction away from You

Listen to the Word of God that He alone is Good and that your salvation is in proximity to Him so sing praise and dance for joy.

He has never failed to liberate the captives and He can lead you home where you belong with Him forever

Slalom Hill Portillo Was North Facing (Pomalift Hill)

In those original days of Portillo Ski Hotel, Chile there was a smaller lift near the hotel itself the slope of which faced northward into the sun and so the snow conditions were usually corn snow and slush with a few bare spots where the Andean brown rocks poked through.

On days when there was a high avalanche danger the main single chairs were shut down and there was only this little bump of a hill a few hundred feet high for the guests to ski. It served as a beginner hill but was often so icy that my soon to be stepmother Dorothy felt quite uncomfortable in her wide apprehensive snowplow at its base: she was just not a skier with no motivation other than to please my father in her futile attempts at such so that he would take her to Davos and St. Moritz, Switzerland on business trips overseas.

My newfound friend John Stirling who was there in Portillo with his archeologist parents from Florida, Aspen and California(all three how nice)was there on the Poma Hill as we called it because the German pilot said we could run slalom with his son Henry and he would time all our runs with a stopwatch. He stood at the base of the hill on his one ski with arm crutches as he had just one leg this older guy but his son had two and it became clear that he hoped his son who was about John Stirlings age six years older than me would be inspired enough to outdo us both but not much luck at that as we were both beating him until one run he did beat John barely by a tenth of a second. We were amused by this fellows attempt in light of his father yelling at him scolding him to the point the poor young man was ready to quit altogether in frustration.

That poor young man was not poor at all and was going to Middlebury College while claiming to be ranked fifth in slalom I'm the East(USA). But in the hotel he confessed to me his father had been a Nazi pilot and I said well my father is Jewish and then he said pulling out a Lugar,

"I shouldn't have told you, now eat this pill it will help you forget!" I fell asleep and probably did forget for a little while but then we were all out there running slalom again with our coach Egon Zimmerman of Lech who wanted us to schuss the hill straight in his tracks through the one foot of deep snow as we would thus not have to climb up the slight hill to the hotel which is surrounded on all sides by fifteen thousand foot high cliffs I almost forgot to mention how steep the Andes are there in Portillo but there are flatter spots and gullies to ski as well.

I was to go last as per Egon's instructions and so I did finally with an uneasy feeling that was justified as when I approached below at almost fifty miles per hour suddenly there was a tall man blocking my path so I veered and crashed narrowly missing some rocks. Everyone came to see me as I was knocked out unconscious but awoke slightly being lifted into the toboggan and into the hotel I was carried to my bed with a serious concussion, I was asleep to long and sobbing miserably and my father's ski instructor Miki Hutter of Salzburg and the paper Nachwritten came to the room with my father and he said,

"You will have to wake up or you will go into a coma and die. So if you want to live and ski some more sit up and get dressed we will walk you around. I acquiesced

St. Ullrich

It was 1916 in the small hamlet Konrads Walau, Silesia a province of Prussia united to Germany back in 1871 by Otto Von Bismark, German Emperor, that Frau Rudel Marthanee Muckner gave birth on July 2 to Hans Ulrich Rudel. His father and grandfathers both Johann Rudels were both Lutheran ministers and he was raised in several parishes where hopefully he might follow in the religious family tradition but he excelled in sports not school.

Ulrich was the name of a saint of Augsburg born 890- and the name means Powerful Heritage which would typify him. Religion was strongly embedded in the Rudel family and it was thought young Hans might be a minister as he seemingly had little interest in women but then he met his fiancé Hanne who seemed so very different. Her great grandfather in fact was Juden or at least half Juden. But those were triumphant people of the Bible and Yahweh their God always was coming to rescue them and the family acquiesced and Hans was permitted to marry the strange young lady. He always liked strange women this continued all his life.

And then came Hitler with all his promises to restore Germany from its defeat in the Great War of 1914-1917 and Hitler insisted that the Juden were to blame for all the world's problems and specifically German problems and that science demonstrated that the people to the East Slavs were an inferior race and that war was inevitable for all great people, the Germans being the very greatest. So Hans volunteered after high school graduation to become a pilot in the Luftwaffe but at Graz he seemed unable to learn new aviation techniques so was promoted but transferred to reconnaissance school and flew a deep mission during the invasion of Poland 1939. He preferred to be in the mountains skiing in his youth but now this was war he had grown up and those Mongols the Ivans had broken their truce with the Fuhrer and Germany so they were now the enemy as well as England even though Silesia had been overrun and pillaged by the Mongol Batu Khan in 1371 the women being raped and there being some Mongol blood possibly inside him as well but no this is not worth considering while the Ivans are inferior like large apes the babies or eggs of the Stuka (Stork)must be dropped exploding among those cave dwellers the Soviets as this was Gotterdammerung Goddamned Warhell! He had transferred out of reconnaissance to Stuka pilot successfully just before the war on the Eastern front and things were going well for him he was destroying many tanks with his new cannon equipped Messerschmidt 109 when suddenly the hero of the Soviet Union came up behind him to shoot him down Rudel dove and swerved between trees as his tail gunner fired in any case the Russian crashed and was missing in action.

The story I heard from Duke whose real name was Gordon was that Rudel had a wife who was one eighth Jewish (Juden) and that because she was married to a living German officer they would not take her to the sterilization delousing camps. Luckily God was with her and him too maybe even Yahweh. He sensed that perhaps after a thousand sorties missions and then as he passed two thousand missions the Ivans firing at his plane usually hit the second plane not him and he kept losing his seconds of wing command then he finally was shot down near the Dneiper river close to the Rumanian border was captured but knowing there was a price on his head attempted escape was shot but swam seven hundred yards across the Dneiper River in winter his tail gunner drowning in the attempt from so much cold. Then he played possum pretended to be dead among all the dead as the enemy searched for him so he survived and was decorated again and flew to defend Berlin in the final days of the war when his leg was hit by fifty caliber and had to be amputated bandaged so he was taken to the Fuhrer Bunker in Berlin where they carried him down the stairs to see the German God Hitler who presented him with the highest medals in a Nazi Propaganda film I managed to see finally at 3 am on the history channel,

"Now Hans if I am no longer Fuhrer will you step up and take command and assume responsibility for the German people?" Hitler goaded him

"No mein fuhrer it would be far better for me to stay in my plane and protect Germany from these barbarians from the east, I must fight on until we will defeat them.

Deliverance.

"Adolf Hitler ist Caput. Deutschland ist Caput!" the radio announced the death of Hitler and the people wept and were in shock but it was too late to save sixty million people who had died and none of these wept. Four Junkers took off in Bohemia and landed at Kitzingen Airfield near Franconia held by the Americans. Rudel had brought his remaining pilots and planes to be captured by the Western allies rather than the barbarous Ivans who wanted his head and Hitler's to be put on posts in Moscow.

Even our enemies are to be considered to be of Saintly importance because they shape us mold us to the task at hand; because without a battle there is no courage to be found anywhere. In times of great prosperity, small men rise to power. Even God wants to correct such imperfection and sends wars and calamities, droughts and plagues, to temper His Earth to righteousness and grace. Be thankful to Him for everything that happens and know peace.

Dear God Three

Our very dearest One and only God our Creator

Quite possibly you are referred to and worshiped in many tongues and languages

You connect us all through Your Love so why do some men doubt You and deny You

Would I be so arrogant as to destroy my own life you have given me?

So please restore to me a day of my own youth and exuberance in my old age

Let me skip and run with joy like a young puppy and let my heart fly like a hummingbird to every flower

That I may exalt Your name in every far corner, on every hill and dale

For You alone are my God, my refuge and rock of salvation

I hold my pen and You alone tell me what to write

Others can write garbage and nonsense to flatter themselves for their advancement

Nevertheless I know it is You Who sustains me and makes my blood to flow from my hand to my foot

Therefore I am no great man at all as I am humbled before the Almighty You

I am of no great importance and I am no president of anything as You Alone are the President of Everything

What are Your Orders of this Your New Day I beseech You to open my ears and hear

Let my eyes behold Your Magnificence at work in Your Creation

Everything You do is Your Perfection and what I do is all in vain until I bow down

I supplicate myself and pray for direction on the highway straight unto You

The road to Jerusalem to see You in Your Holy City and to stand there

Because You wash my feet and clean my heart and lead me away from the defilement

Sodom and Gomorrah are behind me, a smoking ruin have seen

The Glory of the Coming of the Lord, You set a banquet Table before me

Where Your Blood is now wine and Your Body is now bread, I am made rich in You

Because of You I am in abundance and prosperity for without You I am lost and in despair

So that You Alone are my God, there is no other, please have mercy upon all of us who acknowledge that You are our God, protect and deliver us from evil, Amen

Now That God Is Dead

Now that God has died

To be resurrected in heaven, a better place

He lived a very full and complete life

To accomplish everything he set out to do.

When I was a small child almost four

I swung up into the apple tree

That long since has died

My mother on the terrace said to my father

"Do you think he is a special child?" to which my father replied,

"Yes he is probably the Messiah" at which they both laughed quite heartily

Over a cocktail or too on that Sabbath morning.

My father's bookkeepers made up a nickname for him at the accounting and investments office,

CHAIRLIFT PHILOSOPHER

They called him God. Of course he was not really so deified

Except in my own mind for I thought he would never die.

Then somehow I missed his one hundredth birthday but visited him a few months after.

He apologized for his poor health and inattention

Yet was quite attentive to television and the news.

He didn't like Donald Trump our president although

Sometimes he found him to be entertaining, a real entertainer.

How did such a man become president? The electorate thought him funny perhaps?

They thought the same of Hitler but woke up when the Mongolian Army entered Berlin,

End of the party. Even the end of Hitler in his underground bunker

Set deep within his own hell, a personal cell.

My father lived through that war as a weatherman for the United States Navy.

Three Messerschmidts dived bombed his platoon in North Africa killing three.

However "God" remained unscathed as usual and he returned stateside to marry very well as they used to say

When the bride's family owned a shoe business or a railroad or several oil wells.

My mother spoke of some other people who had,

"More money than God!" which I suppose meant that we didn't have any still.

So we, me and her, stayed home with the Negroes, all very friendly helpful superstitious people,

While my father went to work boarding the commuter train

Which carried him to his brothers' office in Manhattan which had been bought from the native Americans for some pieces of cloth plus beads,

"A very good investment "my father reiterated what had been taught to him in grade school.

He learned quite well and purchased a calendar company to keep track of Time Itself.

My mother, however, did the Ouija board with her friends, some witches.

Then she took an ambulance ride to the Sanatorium in Massachusetts a very distant state where it snows.

I was not permitted to go in the building to see her,

So I played outside her window and climbed the hill with my skis to show off what I had learned.

It was a very upsetting trip, especially not seeing her.

Soon we had a governess living in our house and she, Caroline, had a husband and son too.

There were some dogs in the backyard but the chickens moved away to the pet store.

God continued to work fervently but still made chicken feed which is not very much money.

His brothers isolated him in the back office which was very small with an uncomfortable metal chair and a telephone that never rang, maybe once a day.

"Okay, Louis, you can go home now as we don't need you for anything!"

What a promotion in all that commotion! So he joined the CIA

Interviewed in Washington, DC and then further interviewed in Lexington, Kentucky which had grass that was blue

So God and I got on a plane for Iceland where I was sick at the airport and had to deplane to a medical facility alone

Because my father was told he could not deplane as he was Jewish.

Then we flew to Germany which had been bombed severely.

There were many bricks in the street with people gathering them while smiling at me.

They were happy because the war was over I am told.

Many cement mixers were running and the old men were laying bricks with the mortar

Building a new Germany free from Nazis.

God was there to recruit a few stragglers and send them to Argentina via the Mafia.

Because there were communists to fight all over the world, very atheistic people

Who didn't believe in God or his calendar of events for their denial,

They would be sent to hell or Llao-Llao, a hotel with a jail in its basement for unbelievers

While Hitler himself waltzed upstairs in the grand ballroom,

Otto Skorzeny occupied the basement. Rudel and Mengele came and went.

For those who don't believe in God there is the lugar I was told.

It was in my ear, it was in my nostrils.

I was offered a last cigarette. I protested,

"I do not smoke at all!" My words meant nothing to these people.

Soon after Russian Roulette brains were on the ceiling mixed with blood.

Luckily they were not my own. Where was God all this time?

Someone said he is in his New York office or Washington D.C.

They all laughed. Then they asked the Jewish prisoner his name.

"I am Jesus Christ who has come to save you!" he told them.

They laughed again hysterically but shot him anyway.

"Who are you? "Someone asked me but I was too afraid and could not speak, my hip dislocated, my jaw broken…

The mortally wounded savior picked the lock and we escaped while the Nazis were at a coffee break perhaps upstairs with Hitler or his lookalike

I carried down that beach as best I could but laid him atop a large rock at his insistence.

There he died on the shore of Nahuel Huapi near Bariloche.

CHAIRLIFT PHILOSOPHER

I left him with some fishermen who came from a small boat for him.

The disciples of his they told me to go

I ran down the road but a Porsche found me.

So I returned to Chile and the USA where God bought me a new Datsun.

I drove it up to tree line in Colorado and built a cabin.

The rest is history, you read my book

Judgement Day, Elohim

So Elohim God decided to have a meeting with all his angels and they drew into a very tight circle like a football huddle when suddenly the air was bad, one had farted. This was a big deal in heaven because obviously one of the angels had cheated gone to earth, partied all weekend and eaten pork as well as tossed bacon bits on his after dinner salad plus munched on pork rinds.

"Okay, one of you has been naughty!" said God looking around, but the angels would not tattle tale on one other. Not one of them would confess to the awful crime of eating Boston baked beans after drinking Sam Adams Ale then throwing boxes of tea off the British ships in the harbor of Boston.

"Only one way to solve this," said Elohim God adding," I will send you all to earth and after your entire lifetimes there it will be obvious who is really stinky fails to clean his her room wash dishes, mop the floor do laundry."

So all the angels were incarnated in the flesh. Some were clean and some were a bit smelly but took weekly baths but one angel was a real pigpen, a total badass.

Be careful what you say and what you eat and what you think that you live within the commandments and clean up your act because on judgement day God Elohim is going to flush the toilet and down that thing is not where you want to end up.

Because your lives are like very thin slices of bread in a very giant loaf which has no ending and no beginning and every day is but a small cracker on the table of God, you are no greater than the ants because the ants work together harmoniously which is what you need to learn in order to be skilled angels again and be part of the loaf of creation Elohim has backed up much as a birthday cake just for you as He loves you so much.

I am a jealous God that I am; henceforth worship no other… (The only workable plan and the one road home)

By planning God out of our lives, by forgetting His Divine Plan,

We have opened up that infamous can of worms!

Unhappiness, despair, disappointment, integrated as a result of myriads of illnesses

We are not only fulfilled and made whole by bringing God back into our lives…

We exist in God's great plan in infinity

There is no separate path, because we are on it, for it is the one beneath our feet

Smooth or rocky depending on, for instance,

Whether we accept that Jesus Christ is our Lord and Savior who died for our sins

That our have eternal life through Him is our very own being

Other options seem to present themselves that are never excluded, unless we realize; actualize; and react except to only one apparent path appearing within the truly blessed

Toward our living God solely, otherwise allowing for a flaming sea of destruction

Your personal relationship with your living God is your own knowledge of where you stand

If perchance he is a god of death in which case there is no hope or no such thing at all

Printed in the USA
CPSIA information can be obtained
at www.ICGtesting.com
LVHW040816080924
790137LV00041B/110

9 781954 886148